The Very Bad Day

Written by Mary Packard

Illustrated by Joy Allen

My First READER

children's press®

A Division of Scholastic Inc.
New York Toronto London Auckland Sydney
Mexico City New Delhi Hong Kong
Danbury, Connecticut

Library of Congress Cataloging-in-Publication Data

Packard, Mary.
  The very bad day / written by Mary Packard ; illustrated by Joy Allen.
      p. cm. – (My first reader)
Summary: A young girl is having a very bad day, from falling out of bed in the morning to not being able
to find her friends, but when she returns home from a rainy trip to the park her friends are waiting for her.
  ISBN 0-516-24415-9 (lib. bdg.)   0-516-25508-8 (pbk.)
  [1. Luck–Fiction. 2. Friendship–Fiction. 3. Stories in rhyme.] I. Allen, Joy, ill. II. Title. III. Series.
  PZ8.3.P125Ve 2004
  [E]–dc22
                                          2003014067

1 2 3 4 5 6 7 8 9 10 R 13 12 11 10 09 08 07 06 05 04

Note to Parents and Teachers

Once a reader can recognize and identify the 48 words used to tell this story, he or she will be able to successfully read the entire book. These 48 words are repeated throughout the story, so that young readers will be able to recognize the words easily and understand their meaning.

The 48 words used in this book are:

a	friends	left	see	want
and	good	me	she	was
are	had	my	stubbed	way
bad	head	not	sweater	went
banged	here	of	the	what
bed	home	on	to	where
come	I	out	today	woke
day	is	park	toe	wrong
did	Jerome	play	up	
fell	Katie	put	very	

I woke up today and fell out of bed.

I stubbed my toe.

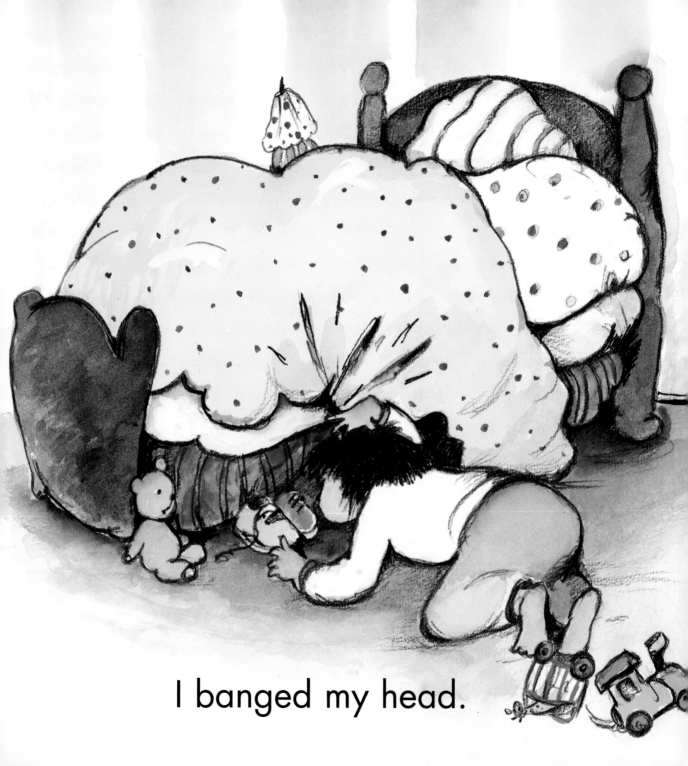

I banged my head.

I put my sweater on the wrong way.

Today is a very, very bad day.

I went to see Katie,
and she was not home.

13

I went to the park and
did not see Jerome.

Where are my friends? I want to play.

17

Today is a very, very bad day.

I left the park. I went the wrong way.

Today is a very, very bad day.

I went home, and what did I see?

Jerome and Katie
had come to see me!

27

Jerome and Katie
are here to play!

Today is a very, very good day!

ABOUT THE AUTHOR

Mary Packard has been writing children's books for as long as she can remember. She lives in Northport, New York, with her family. Besides writing, she loves music, theater, animals, and, of course, children of all ages. When they read *The Very Bad Day,* Packard hopes that children will take comfort in the fact that everyone has a bad day sometimes and that books are an excellent way to share in the human experience.

ABOUT THE ILLUSTRATOR

Joy Allen has loved drawing all her life. She attended Choinards Art Institute in Los Angeles, California, for a year before getting married and starting a family. Allen is the mother of four grown children and has two grandchildren, who appear in some of her books. In four years, she illustrated thirty-two books, including picture books and early readers. She lives in California.